Victim or Survivor

by
Sue Denney

CrossBooks™
A Division of LifeWay
1663 Liberty Drive
Bloomington, IN 47403
www.crossbooks.com
Phone: 1-866-879-0502

© 2012 Sue Denney. All rights reserved.

No part of this book may be reproduced, stored in a retrieval system, or transmitted by any means without the written permission of the author.

First published by CrossBooks 4/26/2012

ISBN: 978-1-4627-1502-2 (sc)

Printed in the United States of America

This book is printed on acid-free paper.

Any people depicted in stock imagery provided by Thinkstock are models, and such images are being used for illustrative purposes only.

Certain stock imagery © Thinkstock.

Because of the dynamic nature of the Internet, any web addresses or links contained in this book may have changed since publication and may no longer be valid. The views expressed in this work are solely those of the author and do not necessarily reflect the views of the publisher, and the publisher hereby disclaims any responsibility for them.

Contents

Victim of Stature	3
Joseph, Son of Jacob	5
Joseph Living in Egypt	7
Joseph Is Remembered	9
Joseph In Charge of Egypt	11
God Has a Plan	13

Victim of Stature

I am 4 foot 11 inches tall, a victim of short stature. I depend on stools, ladders, and tall people to reach items that are too high for me to reach. I will always be a victim of short stature.

One of my favorite stories in the Bible is the story of Zacchaeus, a wealthy man and chief of tax collectors. He too was a victim of short stature. One day he heard that Jesus was coming to town. He realized that the only way he was going to see Jesus was to climb into a sycamore tree. Sitting in that sycamore tree, a victim of short stature, Zacchaeus was given a chance to become a survivor. Jesus told him to come down from the tree and take him to his house. During supper, Jesus gave Zacchaeus a decision to make that would change his life forever.

Zacchaeus was still a victim of short stature but became a survivor serving God. Zacchaeus made a decision to change his reputation of a dishonest tax collector by giving half of his possessions to the poor and paying back those he had cheated by four times the amount he had taken from them. Zacchaeus would always be a victim of short stature for there are some things in life you cannot change.

The day Jesus went to Zacchaeus' house, he quit being a victim of dishonesty and unbelief and became a survivor by trusting Jesus as his Savior.

Joseph, Son of Jacob

Now Jacob loved Joseph more than any of his other sons, because Joseph had been born to him in his old age; and he made him a coat of many colors.

When Joseph's brothers saw that their father loved him more than them, they hated Joseph and could not bring themselves to speak peaceably to him. Genesis 37:3-4

Joseph was a victim of his brothers' jealousy, Joseph had no control over how his father treated him differently from his brothers.

Victims of childhood abuse, rape, and domestic violence have no control over their abusers. Joseph didn't ask to be his father's favorite son. It wasn't his fault his brothers were so jealous of him.

Victims of childhood abuse, rape and domestic violence don't ask to be sexually abused and physically harmed while living in fear for their lives. It is not their fault.

Joseph Living in Egypt

One day Joseph brothers saw a chance to get rid of him. They sold Joseph to some men going to Egypt. Joseph continued to be a victim of his brothers' jealousy.

In Egypt Joseph became a slave to Potiphar, an officer of Pharoah, ruler of Egypt. Joseph continued to be a victim. He didn't ask to be a victim of slavery. Victims of childhood abuse, rape, and domestic violence don't choose to be victims of their abusers. Joseph's life was changed forever when he became a slave to Potiphar.

Victims of childhood abuse, rape, and domestic violence lives are changed forever. Their freedom is gone and they become slaves to their abusers.

Joseph continued being a victim of slavery. Lies were told against him and he ended up in prison. When a person is abused the devil tells lies to them that it is their fault and no one cares about them.

Joseph sat in prison because he was forgotten by the one that claimed to care about him. He continued to be a victim, an innocent victim that no one remembered.

Victims of childhood abuse, rape and domestic violence sit in the prison of life wandering if anyone will remember to care about them.

Joseph Is Remembered

Pharoah had a dream that made no sense to him. He called in the dream interpreters but no one could tell him what his dream meant.

The person who had forgotten Joseph in prison suddenly remember that Joseph had interpret a dream for him and it came true. He told Pharoah about Joseph and his ability to interpret dreams. Joseph was able to interpret Pharoah's dream and was released from prison. Joseph was no longer a victim in prison. He was free. He became a survivor.

Victims of childhood abuse, rape and domestic violence can find freedom from the pains of being a prisoner of abuse. They have to relive the pain of their memories. They have to realize it wasn't their fault. They have to realize they didn't choose to become prisoners of abuse.

Joseph In Charge of Egypt

Pharoah put Joseph in charge of the whole land of Egypt. Joseph went about Egypt a free man.

Victims of childhood abuse, rape, and domestic violence don't have to continue living the memories of lies planted by the enemy. Once they are set free of the pain, they can live life with freedom.

God gave Joseph the wisdom to prepare Egypt for hard times. He stockpiled food all through Egypt for the hard years that were coming.

When the rains stopped and the people ran out of food, Joseph opened the storage and began selling food to the people.

One day Joseph saw his brothers in the store where the food was stockpiled. They did not recognized him. Joseph made a choice to forgive his brothers and in time moved his family to Egypt.

Joseph continued to be a survivor by forgiving his brothers. Victims of childhood abuse, rape, and domestic violence who are healed of the pain caused by their abuser, they too must forgive to become true survivors. Victims don't choose to become victims. They have a choice to continue to be victims or forgive their abusers and become survivors.

Joseph chose to forgive. Are you willing to forgive?

Forgiving others as Christ forgave you. Ephesians 4:32

God Has a Plan

God wants you to have a healthy and happy life. You can have a personal relationship by:

Admitting to God that you are a sinner.

Repent: turning away from your sins.

Believe:

By faith receive Jesus Christ as God's Son and accept Jesus gift of forgiveness from sin.

Confess:

Confess your faith in Jesus Christ as Savior and Lord.

If you are choosing right now to believe Jesus died for your sins and to receive new life through Him, pray a prayer asking Jesus to forgive you of your sins and to live in your heart.

For I know the plans I have for you declared the Lord plans to prosper you and not to harm you, plans to give you hope and a future. Jeremiah 29:11

CPSIA information can be obtained
at www.ICGtesting.com
Printed in the USA
LVIC040352080512
280773LV00001B